Balance Your Life and Work

How to get the best from your job and still have a life

A & C Black • London

Revised edition first published in Great Britain 2009

A & C Black Publishers Ltd
36 Soho Square, London W1D 3QY
www.acblack.com

A CIP record for this book is available from the British Library.

ISBN: 9–781–4081–1196–3

This book is produced using paper that is made from wood grown
in managed, sustainable forests. It is natural, renewable and
recyclable. The logging and manufacturing processes conform
to the environmental regulations of the country of origin.

Design by Fiona Pike, Pike Design, Winchester
Typeset by RefineCatch Ltd, Bungay, Suffolk
Printed in Spain by GraphyCems

Contents

What's *your* work–life balance like? iv

1 Weighing up your current work–life balance 1

2 Working out your values and priorities 12

3 Working more flexibly 25

4 Juggling family *and* work demands 40

5 Thinking about the benefits of a career break 51

6 Learning to prioritise 64

7 Surviving stress 74

Where to find more help 87

Index 89

What's *your* work–life balance like?

Juggling lots of commitments means that life today has never been busier. Whether you have family commitments or not, it can sometimes seem hard to fit everything in—we all want to be successful at work and yet have time for ourselves. Work through these questions, to assess your work—life balance, then read the guidance points.

How much of your time does work take up?
a) I let work take up as little time as possible.
b) A fair amount—but I still leave time for myself.
c) Work seems to dominate my life.

What position does work hold in your personal life?
a) Once I'm out of work I forget about it.
b) I do spend some time thinking about work while I'm not there.
c) I think about it constantly.

How often do you find yourself getting swamped by tasks?
a) Never.

b) Occasionally.

c) Often.

How often do you find yourself getting stressed at work?

a) Almost never.

b) Occasionally.

c) All the time.

Be honest! Which of the following best describes you at work?

a) Over-relaxed.

b) Balanced.

c) Workaholic.

Do you feel you have enough time for yourself outside work?

a) Yes.

b) Most of the time.

c) No.

Do you feel like you are in control of your life?

a) Yes.

b) Just about.

c) No—I feel I'm being swept along by work.

Are you happy with where you see yourself in 3 years' time?

a) No. I'd like to have accomplished more at work than I think I will have.

b) Yes.

c) No. I'd like to have more of a life outside work than I think I will have

a = 1, b = 2, c = 3.

Now add up your scores.

- **8–14:** You seem to have plenty of time for yourself, but are you fulfilling your potential at work? Take a moment to work out what is important to you and make sure you're on track to achieving it—chapters **1** and **2** provide advice on this. Creating a list of priorities for the future can help you to set goals for yourself and ensure you don't miss opportunities. Some time away from the office may help you work out what you want to do. Turn to chapter **5** if you're thinking about a career break.

- **15–19:** You appear to have struck a healthy balance, putting in the effort at work while still having the time for 'normal' life. In order to keep this balance and take your work and life in the direction you want, it could be worth creating a plan to make sure you get where you want to be. Turn to chapter **2** for help on this. To keep up the good work, chapters **6** and **7** will help you prioritise and prevent stress building up.

- **20–24:** Your work just seems to have swamped your life. Sit down and take stock of your position, and assess what's important to you. Chapters **1** and **2** will help you work this out. You can then move on to plan how you can change aspects of your life and claw back some time for yourself. Chapters **3** and **5** can give you some advice on this, and chapters **6** and **7** can help you to become more efficient, making your work life a better place to be.

Weighing up your current work—life balance

'Time flies when you're having fun' goes the adage. Time also flies when you're very busy—but rather than having fun, you can soon find yourself stressed in a way that affects not only your mental and emotional wellbeing, but your physical health. When there isn't enough time in the day, something has to give: but is it to be your work or your personal life? Achieving a balance has become one of the burning issues of the day.

Here are some of the main reasons why more and more people are addressing the topic of work—life balance:

- More women joining the workforce means greater demands on parents to juggle job and family.
- More people living longer means that a growing number of workers care for elderly relatives.
- More pressure and longer hours at work on account of modern technology (for example, overflowing inboxes, the deluge of information from the Internet, and ringing phones) mean people 'burn out' younger.

Government figures show that although Britain has the longest working hours in Europe, our workforce isn't as productive as those in some countries with shorter hours. So while people are spending more time at work, they aren't necessarily achieving more.

The broad argument for greater balance and flexibility at work is that greater satisfaction among employees will lead to fewer stress-related illnesses, less time taken off for sickness, lower staff turnover, and higher productivity. People with a good balance between their work and other responsibilities and interests tend to be more motivated and productive: in other words, happy people work better.

Step one: Understand what the concept means for *you*

The ideal work–life balance is a very personal concept. It isn't an obvious, tangible, or static thing that people can identify, get right, and then expect to keep. It's dynamic and has different elements for different people at different times.

Work–life balance is sometimes confused with finding ways to work less or to work flexibly, because for some people these are the most important elements of a good balance. As a general concept, work–life balance is a feeling of being in control of your life, being able to exercise choice, and about finding an equilibrium between your own needs and those of others, whether at work or at home.

If you're unhappy about the way things are for you at the moment, don't worry; there's a lot you can do to help yourself. The first step is to pinpoint what being in and out of balance is like for you and to understand the triggers. Once you've worked out those, you can move on to find a solution.

Step two: List your symptoms of being out of balance

To work out a way to move forward and get your life in kilter, it's a good idea to first look back at how you've felt in the past.

✔ Take a sheet of paper. Remembering the last time you were really out-of-balance, list some words that describe what you felt. For example, you may have felt as if you were spinning out of control, chaotic, panicky, stressed, shattered, or ill.

✔ List how people at work would have described you during this period, and the behaviour they might have noticed at that time.

✔ Now list how your family and friends would have described you during the same period.

✔ Do the same for each out-of-balance episode you can remember.

Step three: Find out what triggers an out-of-balance state for you

Think back through the episodes above when you felt out-of-balance and narrow your focus down. Ask yourself:

- What happened to start each out-of-balance episode?
- Was it an action you took? If so, what triggered that action?
- Was it an external event? If so, what were the first signs of the event?

When you've done this for all the episodes from step one, review your triggers. Are there common themes? For example, did you feel out-of-balance when your boss put too much pressure on you? When you had a row with your partner or with a close friend? Were you already out of sorts before that?

TOP TIP
Close your eyes and take some deep breaths.
Imagine breathing out all the negative
or stressful thoughts that you've
been remembering. Take a break
before moving on to step four.

Step four: Work out how you feel when you're *in*-balance

Perhaps surprisingly, describing being in-balance is not always easy. It changes according to who you are, what's happening, and when.

✔ Take another sheet of paper. Remembering the last time you were really in-balance, list some words that describe what you felt. How will you recognise that feeling again?

✔ List how people at work would have described you, the behaviour they might have noticed during this period.

✔ Then list how your family and friends would have described you during the same period.

✔ Do the same for each in-balance episode you can remember.

Step five: Find out what triggers an in-balance state

✔ Now review each of these pleasant periods and try to identify what happened to start each period. Ask yourself:

■ Was it the result of an action you took? If so, what triggered that action?

■ Was it the result of an external event? If so, what were the first signs of the event?

✔ When you've done this for all the episodes from step three, review your positive triggers. Are there common themes?

TOP TIP

It's good to feel in control; some people call it 'being in the zone'. Whenever you think that sensation is slipping and you need a lift, close your eyes and remember how you feel when you're in the zone. See if thinking about one of the positive triggers helps you tip you back into your balance zone.

Step six: Work out how you feel at the moment

Now you've identified what the ends of the spectrum are like for you, you can 'map it out' in a simple table or grid. Add descriptive words from steps one to five in the bottom line, as you'll see in the example overleaf.

Totally in balance	Tipping in	Neither in nor out of balance	Tipping out	Totally out of balance
In tune with me and family, happy, relaxed, confident, generous with my time, proactive.	Kind to myself, take time out, even cancelling work, make more time for family.	Indecisive, reactive, not very kind to myself, perfection-ist, OK with others.	Unkind to myself, don't rest, take on too much, pile on the pressure, snappy with my kids and partner.	Hate myself, rude / unfair to others, exhausted, defensive, ill, no sense of humour, depressed.

When you've put in your own descriptive words for each part of the spectrum, you can identify the 'box' that best describes your current state. You can use this personalised tool to tune in regularly. If you are tipping out of balance, you'll find that you see the warning signs earlier; this will help you to take some remedial action before things get really difficult to deal with.

Step seven: Find your locus of control

One of the key themes in work—life balance is your locus, or centre, of control. Again, this isn't a static factor but one that can be changed by beliefs and by events. When people feel in control, they can 'make things happen' and psychologists have shown that feeling in control is associated with a better sense of well-being. When people feel like this, they're said to have an *internal* locus of control.

When people feel controlled by others or by events, things are happening *to* them and they're said to have an *external* locus of control. They're more likely to feel anxiety, loss of confidence, and report physical symptoms of stress. In the extreme, an external locus of control can lead to a long-term state of helplessness and depression.

A locus of control is best thought of as a ratio, because it isn't the same across all situations. To identify whether your locus of control is generally internal or external, keep a diary for a week. Each day, think back over the different stages, tasks and meetings of the day and identify how in control you felt. You need to suspend your logic; what you are doing is honestly recording how you felt. Here's a worked example:

Part of day	*Internal* **I was making things happen**	*External* **Things were happening *to* me**
Getting up	✔	
Taking children to school		✔
Getting to work		✔
Organising my day		✔
Meeting with staff	✔	
Responding to clients		✔
Solving problem	✔	

Part of day	Internal **I was making things happen**	External **Things were happening *to* me**
Lunch	✔	
One-to-one with boss		✔
Out on client site with boss		✔
Picking up children		✔
Making tea	✔	
Going to the gym	✔	
Bath and bed	✔	

In this example, the person recording their locus of control has a 50:50 ratio. As we don't know what's right for that person, we can't tell if that ratio in this case is good or bad. What you need to do, once you've worked out your current ratio, is plan what you'd like it be in the future. For example, you may be comfortable with a different ratio at work from at home. If so, which ticks would you transfer between columns?

TOP TIP
Review the steps above and make a list of
what you would like to change for the
future. Carry this list forward to the
next chapter, to work out your priorities.

Common mistakes

✗ You feel trapped

If you allow yourself to believe that you can't change anything, you're ignoring a huge array of everyday choices that you make through habit alone. Suspend this belief while you go through these exercises, deciding instead what you would like to change 'if you could'. Allowing yourself to visualise the future you want is an incredibly positive exercise. By the time you've worked through the steps in this book, your belief will be more along the lines of 'I choose to . . .'—*you'll* be making things happen.

STEPS TO SUCCESS

✔ Work–life balance means different things to different people; what's right for you might not be the right thing for others, even those you're very close to, such as friends, family, or your partner. Don't make any assumptions about the right balance for other people; they need to work it out for themselves.

✔ Work–life balance is also dynamic; the right balance for you will change as you go through your life.

✔ If you're a manager and you're worried about the work–life balance of one of your team, talk to them about it. Listen carefully and don't leap in with advice or jump to the wrong conclusion when you have no evidence.

✓ Learn to recognise what being in-balance or out-of-balance means to you, so that you can quickly take steps to remain in your personal balance zone.

✓ Understand what triggers different states of balance for you. This will help you to predict periods of stress and work on contingencies in advance.

✓ Assess your current state of balance regularly and work out what you'd like to change. This increases your locus of control and by being proactive, you'll stay in your comfort zone.

Useful link

The Work Foundation:
www.theworkfoundation.com

Working out your values and priorities

In Chapter 1 we looked at how to assess your life balance and having done that, you should have a clearer picture of what is working for you currently and which areas of your life you would like to change. You also have a better understanding of what being in or out of balance is like for you, and this will help you recognise the symptoms early and take steps. Hindsight is wonderful. It's relatively simple to look at the past and even the present and say what is right for you now. It's harder to look forward and decide what balance will be right for you next week, next month, or next year.

Knowing what the balance is that you're aiming for and trying to maintain is the starting point. The steps below will help you to break down what the factors are and to organise yourself according to their relative importance to you. In fact, what will be right for you tends to change, so you need to make time to check it and adjust it if things have changed. Add a weekly 15-minute check in your diary every week until it becomes a habit.

Step one: Work out what's important to you

Divide up a page into the following areas:

- Me
- Partner / Family
- Work / Career
- Finances
- Friends / Hobbies / Leisure
- Health

Write down the things that you feel passionately about in each of these areas. You may find that there are a lot of overlaps, and you may also find that some boxes have lots in while others have very little. Don't worry about this—there are no hard and fast rules.

Real life example 1

Me	Earn respect. Be loving. Don't hurt others. Space and downtime for me. Learning and growing. Time to sit and think. Recharge batteries.
Partner / Family	Love. Two-way support. Time together. Teamwork. Atmosphere.

Work / Career	Earning. Integrity. Professionalism. Collegiate atmosphere. Challenges. Lots of interaction with people. Building something for the future. Being respected. Having a good reputation.
Finances	Earning enough to be comfortable. Planning ahead. Investing wisely where possible.
Friends / Hobbies / Leisure	Lots of interaction with people. Holidays with others.
Health	Fitness. Good physical appearance. Good mental health.

If you find this difficult to do, here's another way of getting at your values.

✔ Close your eyes, imagine yourself at a much older age, looking back at your life. First, imagine that you've had a really full and satisfying life. Take a sheet of paper and write down the things that you're proud to have done. What were the best bits that give you joy to remember? Now imagine that you're looking back over a wasted life. What do you regret and what do you wish you had done more of?

Real life example 2

Time and energy well spent in a full and satisfying life:

- My family: time spent talking, communicating with them, helping them develop, just being together, loving and being loved.
- Building solid friendships for love, sharing, support, and learning.
- My business: created something bigger than myself, developed great understanding of clients' needs, developed new ways to help.
- Helping others.
- Developing myself to understand others better.

In a wasted life I would regret:

- Not travelling and learning about other cultures.
- Wasting time on appearances rather than substance.
- Lost contacts with family and friends.
- Staying employed all my life for the 'security'.
- Wasting my creativity.
- Harming others or failing to help where help was needed and I was able.
- Poor health as a result of not looking after my body.

Step two: Translate these thoughts into a single list of your values

✔ Write, in a couple of words, the essence of each of the thoughts you've listed in the previous exercises, with no repeats. Sometimes two or three of your original thoughts might be summarised under a single heading.

TOP TIP

Values are very personal and so are the definitions that we use. Don't worry too much about the words that you use here; other people may interpret them differently, but that doesn't matter. The important thing is that *you* know what you mean by a particular label.

For example, the labels you could use are:

- Love and fun
- Respect
- Harnessing thought and creativity
- Development and support (self and others)
- Communication and interaction
- Earning / being productive
- Helping others
- Building for a better future

Step three: Work out the relative importance of these values to you

Values tend to be hierarchical, which means that you can prioritise them. As the next step in the process, rank your values in order of their importance to you.

TOP TIP
For you to get the best out of the exercise,
don't allow any values to 'tie' (that is, be
joint first, joint second, and so on); the list
has to be a real rank in order of importance.

For example:

1. Love and fun
2. Respect
3. Building for a better future
4. Helping others
5. Earning / being productive
6. Development and support (self and others)
7. Communication and interaction
8. Harnessing thought and creativity

✔ To check that the order you've chosen is right for you,
   ask yourself: 'If I have value no. 1 (in this case, love and
   fun) in my life, will I have value no. 2 (respect)?' And so on
   down the hierarchy.

✔ If the answer is 'yes', then they're in the right order for
   you. If the answer is 'no', try a different order, until each
   pair feels right.

TOP TIP

It may seem that logically your values might
not be linked in this way, but try to suspend
your logic while you try the step above.
Values are internal and sometimes
irrational, but there is a 'natural' order
to them. Clarifying the hierarchy of
your values is a very powerful step
in helping you to prioritise in a way
that is more satisfactory *for you*.

✔ The second check is to start at the bottom of the
hierarchy and ask: 'Does value 8 (harnessing thought
and creativity) support and contribute to value 7
(communication and interaction)?'

Because the relationships between the values are based on
your beliefs about living, others may not find them strictly
logical or make any sense of them. As long as they make
sense to you, though, you'll derive benefit from them.
Remember that your beliefs are built up from a very young
age as you learn from your experiences. As you work
through this exercise, you may experience moments of
insight about why certain elements of your life balance are
the way they are. For example, if you shared the values
displayed in the examples above, you may find that your
great drive to 'build a better future' is fuelled by the belief
that this will contribute to 'respect' and therefore allow you
to 'be loved and have fun'.

Step four: Set yourself some goals

Now you need to bring the results of the exercises into the real world and translate them into positive action.

✔ With your list of values in front of you, ask yourself what you'd like your life to be like in 3 years' time.

✔ Write your answer in the positive present tense, making sure that your answer is as fully descriptive and as positive as you can be.

You may end up with three or four bullet points for each value. Some of these may be statements about things that you regularly do, others may be specific qualifications achieved or goals met. Include how you'll feel about your achievements.

For example:

Value: love and fun

The family eats together most evenings and we chat about our day and our plans freely. There are lots of laughs and genuine contact between us. We set aside time for homework and encourage the children through our example, sitting down with them where possible. At weekends I spend plenty of time playing with the children and finding new ideas or environments to introduce to them. We also allow them time without direct supervision.

My partner and I make time to relax together and just be in each other's company, whether with friends or alone.

or

Value: interest

I go for lots of walks with no pressure of time at weekends, and enjoy the house and local countryside. I feel really fit and in tune with the seasons. I can consider investment projects and get through the reading I want to do. I spend lots of time on creative things, such as painting, music, and socialising.

TOP TIP

Don't forget to include elements that you identified as things you wanted to change when you worked through the exercises in Chapter 1.

When you read back through your 3-year plan, it should feel inspiring. When you read it, it should make you feel, 'Yes, this is what I am working towards'. If it doesn't, go back through your values and see which is not fully implemented in your plan.

✔ Once you're happy with the 3-year statements do the same for 1 year's time. Bear in mind that three 1-year plans must add up to the 3-year plan.

✔ Next, plan for 6 months' time, again in the positive present tense. Remember to make this realistic and in tune with the 1-year plan.

✔ Finally write your 1-month plan. You could turn some elements of this plan into a diary, if you find that helpful. Make sure that you're as positive, clear and descriptive as you can be about what you've achieved by the end of the month. Be careful about the goals you set, though, and plan in advance how much progress is 'enough'. There are only 24 hours in a day and you may not be able to fit everything in. Remember to give yourself a break even as you work towards achieving your goals. If you don't think your plan is realistic, think back over the long term. Ask yourself:

■ which opportunities are only available now?
■ which things can take a back seat for the moment without negatively affecting my life balance?

TOP TIP

The 3–1–6–1 plan is very powerful and can act as a fantastic motivational tool too. As you work through the steps, you'll become very clear about, and very active in, the choices you're making and this will help you feel more in control of your destiny and your balance. When you feel your motivation dipping or your balance slipping, refer back to your plan and review the choices you've made. Are they still right for you or should

---

something change? Remember that the
plan's not set in stone; it's just a way of
laying out what you're hoping and working
for. Make it flexible so that when *you*
change (as we all do), your plan will
also change. Review the plan each
month and write the next month's.

Common mistakes

✗ You confuse other people's values for your own

When we're young we learn a lot from our parents,
siblings, teachers, and other people with prominent
roles in our lives. We also take on others' values. Later,
as we become more independent, we may test and
throw out some of what we've learnt and we go through
a transition period during which our adult 'persona' is
formed. Adults often carry with them the 'voices' of
important others, reminding them of 'musts', 'shoulds',
and 'oughts' and sometimes people find these useful.

Be aware of these voices as you go through the steps in
this section. Do you *really* agree with them deep down?
Are still they helpful to you? Or have the 'oughts' and
'shoulds' become tyrannical, pushing you to do things
that aren't resonant with your values? Watch out for
times when you use these words and ask yourself if
they're coming from within you or from others. Are
they right for you?

✗ **You don't take into account other people's needs**

Although the process outlined above focuses mainly on you and how you think and feel about things, do check in regularly with the important people in your life as you work through it. Perhaps they'll want to think about their values too, so that you can see which are truly compatible and where important differences lie. Don't see this as a threat to your relationship with them, but rather as a way to help you to appreciate each other's positions better in the future. Your plan may very well require support or direct input from these people, so it will be important to see whether your plan takes their needs and timings into account. For example, if you have a family, the plan has a much better chance of working if you're all on the same wavelength than if you're all planning in different directions.

STEPS TO SUCCESS

✓ Values are the motivational elements that drive our actions and reactions. They're built up throughout our lives and have been shown to work hierarchically. Knowing the relative importance of your values can give you great insight into why you act and react the way you do.

✓ Create a plan that includes the elements you need to have in balance. Setting goals around these elements draws you toward the future you would like.

✔ Others have an effect on our values and on our plans.
  Don't forget to talk to those who share your life.

Useful link

Mind Tools:
www.mindtools.com

Working more flexibly

Chapters 1 and 2 covered how to assess how you feel and what your main priorities are. We'll now look at some of the options open to you to improve your balance and the quality of your life overall.

The good news is that people are much more aware of the importance of a good work–life balance than ever before, and achieving it doesn't mean that you have to change your life radically: it's all about modifying the way you work in order to accommodate other responsibilities or aspirations. It doesn't only apply to parents of young children or people who need to care for dependents, but all of us.

Flexibility in the workplace is being driven by business need—working cultures and attitudes are changing in many parts of the world, and a good deal of employers see the need to adapt to this if they are to recruit and retain the best people. In short, then, you're an asset and your company will want to keep you!

Step one: Find out about the options open to you

Employees now have the right to take periods of paid maternity, paternity, and parental leave, as well as the right to take time off (either paid or unpaid, depending on circumstances) to care for dependents. There are, however, several other key areas in which you can address your work–life balance needs and preferences. These are:

| Flexi-time working

People working on flexi-time schedules are able to vary their start and finishing times, providing they work a set amount of hours during each week or month.

Flexi-time is not only great for parents trying to manage a household as well as a job, but for anyone who finds working within a strict and continuous routine depressing and demotivating. Everyone's energy levels fluctuate during the day but not necessarily at the same time, and so flexi-time is a good solution to making sure people always work at their peak. Another great advantage, particularly for city-workers and commuters, is that flexi-time gives you the opportunity to avoid rush-hour—probably one of the most time-wasting and stressful parts of the day.

2 Part-time working

Employees with a part-time arrangement may decide
between working fewer days each week or fewer hours a day.

This option also works well for people with parental or caring
responsibilities. The other people who benefit greatly from
part-time working are those returning to work after looking
after young children, those recovering or suffering from
illness, and people who are trying to pursue other interests
or careers.

TOP TIP

**Part-time working should be attainable
without becoming side-lined in the
organisation or losing benefits, such
as sick pay and holiday pay. If you're
concerned about this, you can find out
more about your rights as a part-time
employee in the Equal Pay Act 1970, and
get advice from the Equality and Human
Rights Commission
(www.equalityhumanrights.com).**

---

3 Job sharing

This involves two people dividing between them a full-time
workload, with each working on a part-time basis. This is
beneficial if you want to maintain something of your career
while being able to spend more time with your children or to
pursue other interests outside work.

---

4 Home working or telecommuting

Many jobs now involve computer-based activities that can be done as easily from an Internet-linked PC at home or in a remote (telecommuting) facility. This style of working is a boon for parents and carers, but is also valuable for people without those kinds of domestic responsibilities: it allows them to work more productively, especially in tasks that require a great deal of concentration, and uninterrupted peace and quiet away from colleagues, phones, and day-to-day admin. It's unusual for someone to work from home or remotely full-time, but some employers do find it a cost advantage to themselves through the reduced need for fixed office space.

5 Term-time working

This option allows employees to take time off work during school holidays in order to look after their children. This time off is usually taken as unpaid leave, although the salary can be paid evenly across the year. The sorts of employers most likely to operate this scheme are those in industries that experience seasonal peaks and troughs.

6 Other options

The variety of opportunities being adopted by organisations to help you achieve the right balance doesn't stop there. The Department for Business, Enterprise and Regulatory Reform (BERR) website is a good first port of call. In addition to the options outlined above, the following exist:

- staggered hours: staff work to different start, finish, and break times.
- compressed working hours: staff work their total weekly number of hours over fewer days.
- annualised hours: staff have more flexibility about taking time off as working hours are calculated over the year rather than by the week
- shift swapping: staff negotiate their working times and shifts between themselves.
- self-rostering: staff state their preferred working times, and then shifts are organised to accommodate as many of those preferences as possible.
- career breaks: as well as paternity, maternity, and parental leave, staff may also be allowed unpaid career breaks and sabbaticals.
- time off in lieu: staff are given time off when they've put in extra hours at work.
- flexible and 'cafeteria' benefits: staff are offered a choice of benefits so that they can pick those best suited to them.

Step two: Make an application for flexible working hours

I Find out how the processes work

✔ First of all, make sure that you qualify for flexible working arrangements. Most people apply for flexible working because of their family situation. At the time of writing, parents of children under the age of 6, or of less able-bodied children under the age of 18 may request flexible working hours (plans are in train to extend this to children up to the age of 16), but they need to have completed six months' continuous service at the company or organisation in question before making that request. Some organisations may also consider flexible working if you need to care for a dependent adult, such as your spouse, partner, or parent.

✓ Check the employees' handbook or with your human resources department (if you have one) to see what the preferred method of application is. The BusinessLink website has some basic forms that may be customised, so your company may be using these already. If not, most companies would expect a request for a change in working hours to be made in writing. This should be followed up within 28 days by a meeting between you and your manager. Bear in mind that only one application can be made in any 12 month period.

✓ Do some informal research. Once you've checked out your company's policy, speak to friends or colleagues who have applied for flexible working hours or who already are working under a new arrangement. How did the successful applicants approach their request? Are they finding it easier or harder than they'd anticipated to work in a new way? Bear in mind that if your working arrangements are changed, these changes are permanent unless otherwise agreed between you and your employer.

2 Make a persuasive case

✓ Prepare your case and try to anticipate the questions your manager may ask you when you meet to talk about your application. Requests can be turned down because managers fear that flexible working arrangements may affect the business, so be prepared to give well thought-out, positive responses to questions such as:

- Will you still be able to be an effective team member?
- How would a change in your working hours affect your colleagues?
- What will be the overall effect on the work you do?
- How could a change in your working hours affect the business positively?

TOP TIP

Be realistic and also be ready to compromise. A popular way of approaching negotiations of any type is to draw up a wish-list for your successful outcome that contains an ideal solution, a realistic one, and an absolute minimum. If you show that you're prepared to be flexible, your manager may be willing to meet you half-way.

✓ Think about when you would want any new arrangement to start and give your company as much notice as you can. This will convey the fact that you're still committed to the company and are thinking about how the potential changes to your working life will fit in overall.

✔ Stress that the quality of your work and your motivation will not change, even if your working hours do. In fact, you'll be more productive as you'll suffer from less stress and will need to take fewer days off sick to look after your children or dependents when they're ill. You could also explain that as part of a reciprocal arrangement whereby all parties benefit, you'd be willing to work extra or longer hours in times of heavy demand. Finally, but no less importantly, explain how much knowledge and expertise you've built up while you've been working there and how much the company benefits from it.

TOP TIP
Many companies or organisations will allow you to bring a union representative with you to a meeting to discuss your application. If you do invite one along, make sure he or she has read a copy of your application and any related documents from your place of work so that he or she is up to speed.

---

3 Follow up

According to the BERR guidelines, you should be informed about the outcome of your application within 14 days of your meeting.

✔ If all goes well and an agreement is reached, your new working arrangement and an agreed start date should be set down in writing and copies given to all relevant parties (you, your manager, and the HR department or representative if you have one).

✔ If your request isn't granted, you may appeal within 14 days of receiving the decision. See the BERR and DirectGov websites for further advice on this issue.

Step three: Set up a flexible working system in your organisation

If you're an employer or manager, be prepared for some extra administrative costs involved in, for example, setting up IT equipment at home for employees. But the benefits of retaining skilled and experienced staff should outweigh these costs, not least in reducing the expense of recruiting and training replacements for dissatisfied employees who leave.

Think about the needs of the business

Start by clarifying the most important needs of your business. Flexible working will only be sustainable if it doesn't hinder your business's ability to perform efficiently and profitably.

✔ Speak to your staff to find out how many of them are interested in exploring flexible working arrangements.

✓ Engage staff in thinking about how flexible arrangements would affect the business and customers. Discuss what sort of re-organisation might be involved in new working arrangements.

✓ Ensure that your staff understand what the business needs from them, so that they don't make unrealistic requests about working flexibly.

TOP TIP
If you're an employer worried that your business won't be able to cope if all the employees decide they want to work flexible hours, you can relax. The evidence so far suggests that only a small proportion of people actually take up flexible working options. By consulting with your employees before new arrangements are introduced, you can avoid resentment developing and ensure that flexibility works to everyone's advantage.

---

2 Develop and implement a policy

✓ Formulate a policy on how your business views flexible working. Discuss these ideas with staff as you formulate them, so that they see the policy developing and feel they've been consulted in the process.

✓ Write down a procedure for how you'll deal with requests for flexible arrangements, and how staff performance will be monitored. Make sure everyone is aware of these procedures.

✔ Implement your plans over a trial period.

✔ Together with staff, review how well the process works, and assess the impact of flexible working on the business.

✔ Make necessary changes to your policy or practices; monitor and review these regularly.

TOP TIP
As an employer, the key to making flexible arrangements work is setting and monitoring the workload and tasks for employees working from home. If proper trust is established and workloads or tasks are agreed and monitored, there should be no need for direct supervision.

Common mistakes

As an employee:

✗ **You don't prepare well enough**
As with all types of negotiation, you need to make sure that you've done your groundwork when you make an application for flexible working hours. First, be aware of

BALANCE YOUR LIFE AND WORK

your rights by researching the issue: you might want
to visit the DirectGov website which sets out the rights
and responsibilities of both employers and employees.
Second, check your company's stance on the issue,
making sure you follow the procedures properly when
submitting a written application. When you meet your
manager to discuss the application, stress that your
commitment to your role and the company will not
change, and think through questions he or she might
ask you about the effects of flexible working on your
work load and that of your colleagues.

✗ You aren't flexible

Bear in mind that the legislation relating to flexible
working hours gives you the right to *request* them: it
doesn't mean that your company will necessarily agree
to your application, although they have a responsibility
to consider it reasonably. If you're flexible when you
meet with your manager and open to compromise if
your ideal scenario isn't possible, then it's much more
likely that you'll end up with a result that suits everyone
concerned.

✗ You don't think through all the financial implications

Don't forget that when you reduce your hours, it's
not just your salary that may be affected. Pension
contributions and other benefits may change too. Be
sure that when you take the decision to apply for flexible
working hours, you'll be able to cope financially if your
application is granted.

As an employer:

✗ You try to implement a cultural change too quickly

Moving towards a work–life balance, and bringing about a cultural change for the better, doesn't happen overnight. You should strive initially to create an environment of openness and mutual respect, where individuals gradually begin to feel a growing sense of support and trust. From there you can move towards striving to achieve a proper balance between the demands of your business and the personal needs of your employees. This will give them the opportunity to contribute fully at work while also being able to fulfil family responsibilities, or whatever private needs are most important.

✗ You begrudge employees who want flexible working arrangements

Employees who make choices that support a work–life balance shouldn't feel a sense of disapproval, nor that they can no longer expect to progress within your organisation. It's important to be inclusive and to avoid alienating people with particular personal needs.

✗ You have insufficient contact with out-of-office staff

Staff who aren't in the office regularly may start feeling isolated. You should try to avoid this as a manager, by planning regular feedback meetings in the office, and organising social events to bring staff together from time to time.

STEPS TO SUCCESS

✔ Research shows that flexible working arrangements can be introduced without damaging a business. There's a clear business case for getting the work–life balance right, as people work better when they're happy with their working conditions, and high turnover costs caused by the loss of skilled staff can be reduced.

✔ When assessing your work–life balance, decide upon your career aims and personal ambitions and how long you think you need in order to achieve them.

✔ Find out about all the various flexible working options available. Consider which one would suit the needs of your desired lifestyle best.

✔ An application for flexible working needs to be well researched. You should prepare your case thoroughly so that the employer feels reassured that you have the business's best interests at heart as well as your own.

✔ Employers should take a planned approach to implementing flexible working arrangements in your business, involving consultations with staff to decide on the best policy and process.

✔ Flexible working policy should be implemented over a trial period, and followed up with a review of how it's working and adjustments to ensure that the business continues to function efficiently.

Useful links

BERR:
www.berr.gov.uk
DirectGov (click on 'employment' option):
www.directgov.uk
Flexibility.co.uk:
www.flexibility.co.uk/issues/WLB/index.htm
iVillage.co.uk:
www.ivillage.co.uk/workcareer/worklife
The Work Foundation:
www.theworkfoundation.com

Juggling family and work demands

Whether you're part of a couple or not, as soon as you have children, many aspects are brought into sharper focus and some important decisions have to be made. You need to know how to move forward and you have to be sure that your work–life balance will allow you to enjoy your time at work and at home too.

Working out who is responsible for childcare, household chores, and earning income are the three most obvious decisions required, but they're not necessarily the easiest or most clear-cut ones to take. This chapter takes you through the steps required to work out the best options for you. Once you know what these are, talk to your boss or HR department about changes you need to make happen at work. Employment law is changing fast in the area of parental rights, so use the Web link below to become familiar with what you should be entitled to—don't assume that your employer will know!

If you have a partner, you'll reap most benefits if you *both* think about the exercises below; it doesn't matter if you work through them at the same time or if you do them separately and then compare notes at the end. Whether you're

**parenting together or alone, these steps will help
you to identify the benefits and risks of different
ways of managing your career alongside your
family life.**

Step one: Identify the advantages and the demands of work

✔ Start by thinking about your current or most recent work role. Make a list of what the benefits are for you and your family, such as:

- income
- social interaction
- feeling valued for a worthwhile role outside the home
- keeping career progression going
- keeping skills up-to-date

✔ Next, identify the demands of having such a role. For example:

- requirement to be at work 40 hours per week minimum
- an understanding that you'll be prepared to work 60 hours per week when it is busy (sometimes this is an expectation that is inherent in a company's work culture, rather than a written element of your contract)
- paying for childcare
- giving the job all your attention and energy during working hours

- a certain amount of socialising with clients outside office hours
- weekend preparation time
- commuting. Depending on where you live, this may be up to as much as three or four hours per day.
- making sure you're completely up-to-date with current trends and markets

---

TOP TIP

Although it's easiest to start with current or recent roles, try to think more broadly now about other work roles that you could consider with your current skills and strengths. Most people will stick with what they know, but if the demands outweigh the benefits it would be worth considering other possibilities that are open to you, rather than feeling trapped. Are the demands and advantages broadly the same for other roles or are some quite different?

Thinking over these issues may help you find a new work area where you could have many of the same advantages that you have now, but with fewer or more manageable constraints.

Step two: Identify the demands of family and home

Thinking about your roles in the home as parent, spouse, homemaker, entertainer, and educator, what be will the major demands on your time, energy, and resources? You may want to answer this question separately for different 'chunks' of time; for example, you could divide it up into First year, Preschool, Primary term-time, Primary holidays, and so on. How you describe the demands is entirely up to you.

TOP TIP

Some people find it helpful to base this exercise on the clock and to divide the time into hours and minutes for each task. This helps them work out what they can happily delegate, how much this might cost them, and how much time they should allow for items they would prefer to do personally.

REAL LIFE EXAMPLE

Baby's first year

Parent	Important bonding time, for development.
	Ensure a strong foundation.
	Involvement of one of us with feeding and routines for most of every day.
	Relaxed time for communication.

	Possibly single other carer during first year— maximum of 4 hours per day, 4 days per week.
	Relaxed time for communication.
Spouse	Allow time out for us. 2 hours / week minimum.
	Have time to share and listen properly = not stressed out and not exhausted.
	Each of us having own time for gym or study each week—3 hours per week.
Homemaker	Be able to afford the mortgage on our wonderful house.
	Have enough extra income for comfortable living. Holidays abroad may go on hold for some years, but would be nice. Keep home clean and hygienic—4 hours per week. Tidiness—30 minutes per day. Washing and ironing, 7 hours per week.
Entertainer / Educator	Make plenty of fun, laughs, and interest. Find toys, sights, and sounds to stimulate. Find suitable social environments to join in with regularly—4 hours a week minimum.

Son's reception year

| Parent | One of us always picking up. School run: 30 minutes twice a day. Share and listen during after-school hours and at suppertime. |

	Able to have friends home—important for socialisation.
	Stimulating play and physical activity, getting involved with projects.
Spouse	As above.
Homemaker	Always have good stock of fresh fruit and vegetables, as much from the garden as possible. Creating nice outdoor relaxing and playing area, 1 hour per day. Cook nutritious meals from scratch most evenings. Encourage family to sit down together to eat when possible.
Entertainer / Educator	Similar to above. Support his learning, especially reading practice—30 minutes dedicated time per evening
	French club if we can get him into it this year.
	Swimming lessons—45 minutes per week

Daughter's year one

Parent	As above.
	Help out with French club at the school towards end of the year
Spouse	As above.
Homemaker	Create a nice place to come back to: 1 hour per week. General shopping: 2 hours per week. Share small chores with children as appropriate.
	Send to school with healthy snack.

Entertainer / Educator	Similar to above. Support her learning, homework this year, and take an interest in what she is reading.
	30 minutes dedicated time per evening. French and football clubs.
	Swimming lessons—45 minutes per week.

TOP TIP

Plan ahead some time that you can spend by yourself and for time that you can spend with your partner or close friends. Without these breaks, you risk becoming stressed and snappy and undoing all your good work in other areas. Time out is important for everyone, but especially for those juggling a career and family commitments, so don't think you're being selfish—you're not!.

Step three: Work out which demands are compatible

Now that you have the dual demands in your life laid out, you'll be in a better position to work out areas where your current role is compatible with them and areas where it is not. For example, you might want to be at home in time to pick the children up at 3pm each day, but you may be working in a role with a long commute which makes this impossible. Add up the time and work out whether this entire list can actually fit into the time available.

✔ Make the demands on your time more compatible with your available energy and resources by splitting up the demands so that they become more manageable and by getting help from others if you can. Be imaginative about this and think about solutions such as:

- getting extra help with the children from an extended family member
- sharing the school run with a trusted friend
- paying for help from a childminder, nanny, nanny-share, or nursery
- hiring a cleaner to help with housework, shopping, and laundry
- finding an *au pair* for help with the laundry and to babysit

Step four: Think about the advantages of *not* working

This chapter has started from the perspective of those who want to manage work *and* family together. You can go for a different route, though, and think about taking a career break and staying at home to handle family commitments if you have a partner who can provide the income. The list overleaf shows some advantages to this solution:

- the higher earner continues to earn at his or her maximum level, giving the family the maximum income per hour worked
- each of you has your arena of focus with clearly delegated responsibilities and aren't stretched too thin
- childcare may be so expensive that it all but wipes out the second income anyway
- there is increased time and energy for looking after home, partner, and family

Common mistakes

✗ You don't negotiate

In general, employers are gaining a greater awareness of changing legislation and are becoming more enlightened in their approach to flexible working. However, they may *not* be aware of what your specific needs are and may need to be sold the advantages of the system you're proposing. It's often a good idea to write down what you're asking for, so that you can structure your argument well and also so that the recipient has time to digest the information and give a more considered answer. If the answer is no, ask what flexible arrangements *would* be acceptable and take the negotiation from there. If your employer is unwilling to consider any changes to your working arrangements, take advice about your position from an employment lawyer or from your trade union if you belong to one.

STEPS TO SUCCESS

✔ Start by identifying the demands that you face and what they might be in other roles.

✔ Think about which of these are compatible already and identify changes that will help you.

✔ Consider the advantages of working and make sure you weigh these up carefully against the advantages of a career break.

✔ Work out which childcare and home help options could be right for you.

✔ Identify which working model will suit your family life now and in future years and decide how you can sell this to your employer.

✔ Be aware of your rights: your boss or company may not necessarily be up to speed with the latest developments in employment law! It's a fast-moving area.

✔ Make any requests in writing. This means that you can keep a record of what has been said and when and you're also giving the recipient time to think over what you're saying rather than having to reply on the hoof.

Useful links

Department of Work and Pensions:

www.dwp.gov.uk

DirectGov:

www.direct.gov.uk

Thinking about the benefits of a career break

One way of adjusting your work—life balance in favour of your home life is to take a career break. There are many positive reasons to take some time away from your usual working day and its routine—a new parental role is the most common reason, but study, travel, trying out a business idea, or caring for a sick relative are other positive priorities that trigger people to spend a period away from work.

People may also take a break to get away from the aspects of their career that they enjoy least. Stress and pressure, office politics, and turbulent periods of upheaval can cause all of us to look for a change of scene that allows us to recharge our batteries, look after our health, and remind ourselves of what we really want in life.

If you've planned to take a career break, you've some options to think about once you get back; you might return to your old job or look for a new challenge when you're ready. These days companies are more likely to look on career breaks favourably and indeed an enlightened employer may have a policy that goes far beyond statutory parental rights. Rather than lose the investment already made in your training and

development, they'll agree to career breaks in the hope that their people will eventually return to employment with increased commitment, renewed loyalty, a broader perspective, and additional skills.

Step one: Look at your motives

It's a good idea to step back and take some time to ask yourself why a career break holds such appeal for you. Do you know already what you hope to experience or achieve? What secondary or underlying objectives do you have?

✔ Visualise the beginning, middle, and end of your time away and your eventual return to work. Make notes about how you want it to be in an *ideal* situation, but also think about how it might work realistically.

The main obstacles

Your other priorities are actually the main obstacles. The most common reasons for not taking a long career break are to do with:

- your partner
- your family
- your career
- your house

For most people, giving up work for a period of time means a loss of the income on which they have become dependent.

In general, the younger you are and the less routine your life is, the less inhibited you may feel in taking the plunge. At the other end of the spectrum, there are some lucky people for whom a career break of 12 or 24 months can be managed on savings alone, allowing them to return to pick up their previous routine without any material change.

TOP TIP

It *is* possible to be made redundant while on a career break, although your employer is expected to consult with you and your trade union in the usual way. If your employer decides to select you for redundancy *solely* because you're on a career break, this could be held to be unfair redundancy selection. The length of time you've been working for your employer will have a bearing on the situation. If you have 12 months' continuous service, you're protected against unfair dismissal, including unfair selection for redundancy, and if you have two years' continuous service, you're also entitled to a redundancy payment. A break of one week will break this continuity, except under circumstances where it's customary for

such absence to count for continuity. If,
therefore, you can show that absence
on a career break constitutes such
circumstances, you'd be protected. As
this is a complex area, discuss it with
your employer and ask for a statement about
continuity to be added to any letters regarding
your career break arrangements.

Step two: Prepare to ask your employer

When you broach the issue with your boss, it's important to be clear in your mind about everything you want.

✓ Take along some notes as prompts if you'd find that helpful.

✓ Know what you're asking for, including the length of time away, pay and benefits, continuity of employment, possibility of return to the same role, and so on.

To make the idea seem as attractive as possible, you need to be able to explain what benefits your break will bring both for you and your employer, and prepare a statement about wanting to return.

✓ Make a business case that would encourage your employer to support your request. For example, let's say that you work for a large multinational organisation but that you'd like to spend some time abroad learning Spanish. You could say that the language skills you'd gain on your break would be put to good use when you return as you'd be able to liaise more quickly and effectively with your organisation's branches in both Europe and Latin America.

TOP TIP

Remember that time off doing nothing may not only be hard to sell to your boss, but to prospective employers too, if you plan on changing jobs upon your return. However, having and achieving some valuable personal objectives during your time away may well affect your career for the better. You'll often be perceived with respect (and perhaps a little jealousy) for having the initiative, confidence, and determination to realise a dream. You'll need to make sure that you communicate what you've gained from your break clearly and positively, though. Stress the benefits when you describe what you've been doing and quantify your achievements if you can. For example, if you have management skills and you've been working overseas for a charity, you could say: 'I helped secure finance for a health centre which enabled it to take on three more members of staff and increase its impact in the community.'

You could also find out whether there's a policy that provides for sponsored sabbaticals. Your employer might be prepared to provide what you request, or suggest a compromise.

✔ Be ready to be flexible and to meet your employer half-way. Remember that your request may have come completely out of the blue, so he or she may feel a bit 'ambushed'.

Step three: Be ready in case the answer is 'no'

You have to be prepared for things not going to plan. If this does happen, first of all find out why you've been turned down. The provision of career breaks is purely at the discretion of your employer, but if they're made available only to women, then they're clearly behaving in a discriminatory manner. If other work colleagues have been granted similar time off for parental or study purposes and you haven't been supplied with a satisfactory explanation as to why you have not, you may want to claim a grievance through your personnel department (if your company has one) or your union.

Even though you're bound to feel disappointed at first, look at the positive aspect of your company's decision: freedom. If you're that committed to the idea of the career break, you'll just go anyway, even if your employer won't keep your job open. The obvious downside to your employer of agreeing to a break is that you're obligated to return. You may feel very differently about that once you've been away for a while, so in a way you've been relieved of that decision.

Step four: Consider other ways of achieving your goals

✔ Go part-time. Part-time work can free you up to realise your dreams without having to take such a significant drop in earnings. If you stay with the same employer, it can also give you continuity of routine and of your social network, both of which can help to reduce the stress related to big changes in your life.

✔ Work from home. Sometimes called 'teleworking', this can allow you more time in your chosen environment and it may also give you the flexibility to control when you work. Many people choose this option since it gives them fewer financial headaches than reducing their hours. There's a negative side to it, unfortunately, in that even if you do go down this route, work will still eat up reasonably large chunks of your time and attention and you may feel isolated outside of your everyday comfort zone. It may also mean that you can't spend as much time focusing on the new challenges you're hoping to explore. It's worth spending some time thinking through an average working week and seeing how that might translate to a home-office setting.

✔ Work abroad. This can be a great way to satisfy a craving for novelty and variety while furthering your career ambitions at the same time. It's the best way to master a foreign language and to gain an understanding of a nation's culture, as you're totally immersed in it.

TOP TIP

Don't forget the financial benefits of working abroad: you'll still be earning something, so this is a good way to fund your itchy feet. You may choose to work within your usual field through a secondment or a change of employer, or you may go for a complete change, such as picking grapes or teaching English. If you're an EU citizen, working within other member countries is relatively easy but remember that if you want to go further afield, you'll have to apply for work permits/visas, some of which can be tricky to get hold of. Whatever you do, make sure you have all the necessary documents before you travel to your chosen destination.

✔ Change your employer. This can give you the chance to negotiate terms as part of your contract, with a view to a future break. This works for study breaks and for travel abroad but may not be suitable for parental breaks, the timescale for which may already be dictated! If you (or your partner) are already expecting a baby, changing employer could result in a loss of rights to parental leave. For example, currently all pregnant employees have a right to 39 weeks' ordinary maternity leave and up to 13 weeks' additional maternity leave. You can receive statutory maternity pay (SMP) for up to 39 weeks only if you have been employed by the same employer *continuously* for a minimum of 26 weeks into the 15th week before your due date, however. This may not affect you right at the moment, but it's worth bearing in mind.

Looking for a new role on your return can give you complete freedom, and it's certainly a good option if you're hoping to take an extended career break. It may also be the most suitable route if you intend to retrain, take a completely new direction in your career, or care for children or other family members in the long term.

Step five: Take the plunge

✔ Look back over the notes you took when you were daydreaming about your career break and prioritise your objectives. Which are most important to you? These are the 'core' of what you'll achieve.

✔ Think about the obstacles that may stand in your way and the contingency plans you'll need to make to deal with them. Obviously you can't see all the potential events that may throw you off course, but attempting to identify the most obvious will bring your plan into the real world.

TOP TIP

Taking 12 months, for example, away from your job will not generally leave you with a skills issue. The more technical your role and the longer you spend away from it, though, the more time and effort you'll have to put into staying in touch. Some employers, such as those in healthcare professions, find it so important to retain good workers that they'll not only allow them to take a lengthy break but will fund their skills updates on their return. In other areas, it may be down to you to update yourself. For more specific advice on this area, talk to the relevant managers in your company or organisation or contact an industry body for advice. If you belong to a trade union, they may also be able to help.

✔ Assess the gap between where you are now and where you want to be. Start breaking it up into manageable chunks and then identify milestones along the way. For example, if you're planning a trip abroad, your first 'chunk' is research about your destination(s), and the first milestone is knowing which visas and work permits are required.

Having a plan will help you move efficiently towards your goals, but don't feel you have to stick to it rigidly. You may decide to rethink your objectives as a result of experiences you have early on, so try to remain focused but be flexible too. Once you get used to planning in the way outlined above, you'll find you waste less time worrying or dithering.

Step six: Tie up loose ends

If you decide to leave your current job when you go on your career break, make sure that you leave with the best possible reputation so that you'll get a glowing reference. This will also mean that you can apply to your previous employer for work on your return, if you so wish. If you *are* planning to return to the same role after your break, it's even more important to make sure that tasks are properly completed or handed over efficiently, and that you train your successor as well as possible.

✔ Start making a list of important contacts and duties well in advance of your leaving date to act as a helpful resource to others in your absence. If at all possible, set up a hand-over period so that your successor can see what you do on an everyday basis.

Common mistakes

✗ **You don't keep in touch**

Keeping in touch is vitally important if you want a smooth transition back into your previous role. It's also important if you'll be moving on to a new career. Stay attuned to who's who and catch up with relevant communications in your business or industry. This is much easier to do these days, wherever you are, and websites, company publications, or trade journals can help with this. If you feel it's right for you, and you're taking some time out to complete a course of study, you could spend your holiday time back at work. This will help your finances as well as keep you in the 'loop'.

✗ **You feel trapped by finances**

Working out financial matters can be difficult and painful, but it can be done as long as you're absolutely clear about your priorities. For example, take time to identify where your money currently goes. What could you achieve with a different plan? Weigh up the benefits of continuing as you are, compared to what you might spend on your career break. Are there ways to reduce spending so that you can save for a career break in advance?

Useful links

Careerbreaker.com:
www.careerbreaker.com

DirectGov
www.direct.gov.uk

TEFL.com:
www.tefl.com

VSO:
www.vso.org.uk

Learning to prioritise

Keeping control of tasks is an essential skill to master when you're trying to balance life and work. It will help you in all areas of life and is particularly useful if you decide to incorporate working from home into your new, better balanced regime. Good prioritisation helps you avoid distraction and become more efficient and self-reliant.

Some people naturally like structure in their life: 'control' is one of the 'big five' personality factors that psychologists agree on. If you're high on 'control' and enjoy structure, order, and routines, it's unlikely that you'll struggle with the steps laid out below.

If, on the other hand, you prefer freedom and variety, you may feel constrained by structure and routines and find it harder to follow these steps. Persevere if you can, as you'll really reap some benefits. It might be a good idea to concentrate on using Step one, so that you're at least clear about what you're trying to achieve with your efforts. Learning to prioritise frees up a lot of time for whatever you would prefer to be doing. Use the steps below as a framework and schedule imaginatively, to give you the variety you need in your daily life.

Step one: Decide on your objectives

If you start off by being clear about what you want to achieve, the chances are that you'll succeed brilliantly. There are several levels to this step:

- What do you (personally) want to get out of any particular period of work (say a month, six months)?
- What do your boss/team/clients/company need you to achieve during this time?
- What specific goals do you want to have achieved by the end of this month?

✔ Write the answers to these questions on a sheet of A4. Hang them in a prominent place in your office, ideally where a distracted eye will fall. You can add on an adjacent sheet of A4 your objectives for your life outside work, if you feel inclined to.

You'll probably have several answers for each question, because our objectives are usually plural. If this is the case, you'll need to identify the *relative* importance of each element of your answer; it may help to organise your page with the most important elements first. Next to these will be the answers to the following questions, which it will become habitual to write at the beginning of the working week and day.

- What do you need to get done by the end of this week?
- What do you need to get done today?

These simple questions will light beacons to guide you through the chaos of each day. When faced with requests or demands for your time and attention, ask yourself how they will help you towards your objectives:

- Should I do it now or after more important objectives have been met?
- Is this something I need to deal with today?
- Is this something I need to deal with this week?
- Do I need to sort it out this month?
- Can this go right on the end of my list in case I have time?
- Should I bother with this at all?
- Can I delegate this to someone else?

Step two: Use tools to help you

Although you don't want to clutter up your life even further, there are some tools that can help you live according to your priorities.

Diary

A diary helps you to plan ahead, scheduling specific dates or times for tasks and actions appropriately. It helps you to structure time towards deadlines so that you can monitor interim goals more easily and make sure they're met, with your ultimate goal being to deliver the outcome you want on time.

✔ Divide projects and objectives into constituent parts and place 'milestones' in your diary. Don't forget to schedule in time to meet people as well as time to complete key tasks, or you could risk isolating yourself.

A diary is especially useful to structure your time if you have lots of short meetings or telephone calls or if you need long chunks of time to focus on difficult, complex, or creative work. By communicating your need to your colleagues and concentrating meetings and other work into one section of the day or week, you free yourself to work in a more effective manner.

Diaries now come in the traditional paper format, in software for your PC or notebook such as Microsoft Outlook or in new '3G' formats as part of a mobile gadget with multiple functions. Whilst computerised devices may offer useful features to those who learn how to use them, a paper diary does the job and is unlikely to develop technical trouble, run out of power, or be incompatible with other systems.

To Do list

In its simplest form, a To Do list is a place to record the things you need to do, so that you can tick them off as you achieve them. Software that allows you to add priorities, due dates, and reminders is readily available, for PC, notebooks, or for phones and other mobile devices. Again, the extra features may be nice to have but a simple paper list is fine.

If you're aware that you take on too many tasks, a To Do list may help you to visualise your workload and manage requests more assertively. The most important thing to remember when using a To Do list is your objectives.

✔ Next to each entry on your list give the task a number to reflect the priority of the task relative to your objectives and the other tasks. You can even make your list public so that your boss and colleagues can see the work already assigned and do some of the prioritising for you.

Time audit

This is a backwards look at how you've been spending your time. It's a useful tool to monitor how well you're focusing your time on the objectives you want to achieve.

✔ Looking back through your diary and To Do list, estimate the amount of time that you spent working towards the objectives you set yourself. Do the same for your time and objectives outside work. How does your time allocation tally? What needs to change: your objectives and priorities or your time management?

Project planner

When managing projects, a project planning system can help you to break down a complex system easily into its constituent elements, identify milestones, assign tasks to others, and keep track of progress. This can be done on paper, a whiteboard, or flipcharts, or on a PC or notebook using one of the software tools on the market.

TOP TIP

'Prioritise' is a verb. That means action, not
tools. People can have a very fancy toolkit to
help them sort themselves out, but it'll be no
use at all unless they actually do something
with it. Don't fool yourself that having a diary
and a To Do list means that you're organised.
Even filling them in will not help alone. It's
the discipline of following the schedule in
your diary and focusing on the completion
of each task on the To Do list that will
make you efficient and successful.

Step three: Manage your inputs and outputs

The process of working efficiently comes in managing the
inputs as they happen and remaining focused on the output
of the most important and urgent task.

First and most important: be clear which set of objectives
you should be focused upon now—work or home
objectives. If you work from home, separate your workspace
from your home space as far as you can. Separate work
time from home time, work phoneline from home phoneline,
and work e-mail from home e-mail too. This way you can
protect yourself from the stress of role confusion.

Managing output

Here is a checklist of things to do when you start your work time.

✔ Look up at your objectives on the wall to focus you on what you need to achieve.

✔ Look at your diary and see what you've scheduled and how much time you have spare.

✔ Look at your To Do list and pick out the tasks that are most important and urgent. You can choose to start a long task and finish it on a different day or you may prefer to pick a single task that will fit within the time you have available.

✔ Allow yourself time for interruptions and three or four 10-minute breaks and a longer meal break within a working day. You'll be more focused and effective if you stay fresh. Now you can write your objectives for the day.

Managing input

✔ Make your days more efficient by allocating time slots to post, e-mails, and incoming phone calls.

How you do this will depend on your role, but for most people the post will only need attention once a day.

✔ Sort out your post near the bin, making three piles:

- junk, no pile for this: straight into the bin.
- items to file for reference: put them away directly after opening everything.
- items to deal with immediately: respond to each one quickly and efficiently.
- items requiring more attention: add to your To Do list or schedule specific time in your diary. Don't forget to think about how important the item is to the achievement of your objectives.

E-mails carry the expectation that they'll be seen and dealt with immediately and some may generate more interruptions if left too long—you'll be chased by the people who sent you the initial message, for example. On the other hand, very few roles require people to respond to each e-mail as soon as it arrives.

✔ Turn off your message alert as it will distract you each time you get a new message and allocate a maximum of three slots in the day for responding to e-mail. Early morning mail may be urgent, so start the day with a quick check, check again after lunch and then one last time as you finish work for the day. Use the same 'three-piles-plus-the-bin' system as you did with your post.

How you deal with your phones depends on your role. You may be expected to answer immediately during office hours. Perhaps you prefer to have the variety of contact with others throughout the day and enjoy the social side of the interruption. Some calls may be quickly dealt with if answered immediately, saving yourself and others time.

✔ If your role allows it, try to switch the answer phone on and return calls during allocated slots through the day, as you did with e-mails. Doing this will allow you greater focus on your objectives for the day, making you more productive. You will need to get into the habit of regularly checking and returning calls, though.

Common mistakes

✗ **Your standards drop over time**
You owe it to yourself to put in a full and focused day towards your objectives or it's unlikely that you'll meet them. If it helps, imagine your boss or colleague's reaction to a piece of work you're finishing. Does it do you justice?

STEPS TO SUCCESS

✔ Know what you're trying to achieve. Break down large or vague objectives into smaller and more manageable chunks, making them more achievable. If you have trouble doing this, get help from your boss or a business coach.

✔ Keep the correct set of objectives in mind at all times.

✔ Know your tools and how to use them. If in doubt about the technology, work a dual system approach until you're certain that you can rely upon it.

✔ Build your own way of managing inputs and outputs based upon the suggestions in this section into your routine. Have a schedule that helps you and stick to it.

✔ Be clear about your different roles and try to keep them separate. There will be times when you're required to switch between them but don't allow this to become routine.

✔ If you find you're slipping back into your old haphazard methods, return to this section regularly to remind yourself. If you struggle at first, have faith! Anyone can learn to prioritise but it may take some time for it to become habitual.

Useful link

Mind Tools (time-management tab):
www.mindtools.com

Surviving stress

Regardless of the general balance of your life, there will be times that are stressful. Learning the practical steps to cope with stress is important to help you get through these episodes. It isn't recommended that you accept and try to cope with an everyday pattern of stress over a long period of time, since this can be very detrimental to your health. Get the balance right first and take steps to deal with stress comfortably.

Step one: Identify the main sources of stress

Pressure can be positive, providing challenges and building confidence as you achieve them. How you see the situation can make the difference between whether you experience pressure or stress. It's important to understand which situations you're finding stressful and to identify the elements within them that cause the stress. General sources of stress at work, home, and in balancing different roles are:

- conflict between people
- handling difficult behaviour
- performance worries

- demanding routines
- increased requirements on your attention or time
- financial worries

Identify sources of everyday stress that fit into each of these categories for you and work out how you can eliminate or alleviate it.

Major life changes have also been shown to cause a disproportionate amount of stress, especially where three or more occur within the same two-year period. The most stressful life events are:

- death of your partner
- divorce or separation
- legal proceedings against you
- a prison term
- personal injury
- marriage
- having/adopting a baby
- losing/changing jobs
- retirement
- moving home
- death of family member

Think about the life events that have affected you in the last two years. The process of adapting to these will inevitably take a toll on your welfare, as you understand, respond to, and live with the change. Think about each life event and how you've dealt with it but without dwelling too much upon it. Give yourself plenty of relaxation time for recovery, using it to do something that you enjoy, unrelated to the change you're facing. Many people will be going through similar life changes. Even those who aren't can understand that this is a difficult time for you and will want to help, so don't isolate yourself.

Step two: Sort out stressful relationships

Contact with others is crucial for getting things done at work, but some people are a lot easier to deal with than others. Your support network outside work can help you to deal with pressures and actually reduce your stress, so getting relationships in good working order is well worth doing.

I Criticism

Do you have to put up with a constant stream of criticism or put-downs from one person? People who are always negative about you or your ideas are probably feeling insecure. Reminding others of their faults is used to deflect attention from their own perceived failings. Perhaps they feel their position is threatened or feel that they need to compete with you. People like this may feel frustrated or have low self-esteem, and they often don't like to see others enjoying success or higher self-esteem than them.

✔ When someone makes a personal attack, rise above it and remain cheerful, rather than reacting to it negatively.

✓ Use phrases such as 'that's an interesting perspective' to show that you've heard without agreeing.

✓ Repeat back a negative comment to the person who gave it. Very often they'll notice the destructive effect of their words and will tone down what they've said about you or qualify it. Listen carefully, as this could be useful feedback. Perhaps you've said or done something that they find difficult to cope with.

✓ When your critic uses sarcasm, interpret what they're saying to check what they're implying and then ask 'why do you say that?' to clarify their meaning. This also highlights their negative tactics, which may be enough to stop the behaviour.

✓ Confront persistent critics directly. Describe the criticism you've been receiving, disclose how it makes you feel, suggest what you would like instead. 'You have been sarcastic and critical of me on a number of occasions recently, which I find hurtful. If you have a problem with something I do, come and tell me direct so we can discuss it'.

✓ At work, make a log of events, including your attempts to confront and resolve the problem.

2 Anger

Do you cope well with angry people? Here are a few simple tips that will help you to draw positive outcomes from difficult situations.

✔ Keep calm yourself, concentrate on breathing slowly, listening carefully, and keeping your body language open.

✔ Disarm the immediate mood by responding and showing concern: 'I can see that this has really upset you; let's discuss it so I can understand fully and see what we can do about it'.

✔ If someone is too upset to listen there's little point wasting your energy. Ask them to come back when they've calmed down so that you can discuss their problem properly.

✔ Find a good time and place to discuss persistent anger problems. Warn the people concerned first about what you want to discuss, so they can prepare themselves. Work out why the person uses inappropriate behaviour, what they hope to gain or what their angry tactics have won for them before. Plan what you'll say to them before you challenge their difficult behaviour. Remind yourself they may have a real grievance or frustration that you can deal with.

✔ Describe your observations of the problem and why it causes problems for you and /or others. Explain what you want them to stop and what you would like to see instead. Ask them if there are any problems with making this change and discuss what you can do to help them. Compromise and negotiation may be required for a solution.

3 Dead battery

Can you identify people in your life who act as a dead
battery, draining you of your energy whilst giving little in
return? Sometimes we can simply 'unhook' ourselves from
a negative or an unresponsive person and have less to do
with them. It can be difficult or impossible to do this if
they're in our work team or family. The issue has to be
dealt with rather than avoided. Find or create a good time to
talk to them, preferably with just the two of you and no
distractions. Describe your observations of their behaviour
and disclose how it makes you feel. Explain what you think
would make the situation better and ask them if there are
any barriers to this happening.

Real life example

Harry finds that Peter's withdrawal from usual family
conversations worries him. His attempts to include his
son in what he is doing, or to get conversations going
are met with negativity or silence. Harry worries. Peter is
clearly unhappy and the problem is affecting the family
atmosphere. Harry sends the rest of the family out on
an errand. He describes what he has noticed and how
worried it has made him feel. He describes Peter's former
positive outlook and how great it was to be with him.
Harry asks if there's anything getting in the way of a
return to this. They discuss a particular problem that
was affecting Peter at school and how to deal with it.
Though Harry feels that Peter held a lot back in their

conversation, the progress was a relief and the
atmosphere was immediately better.

Step three: Communicate assertively

Prioritisation and self-organisation can reduce your stress
and help you to manage a demanding workload. In a
nutshell, promising less can mean that you get more done
but what if you find it hard to say no or to ask for the help
you need? As with any skill, practice improves performance,
so here are some exercises that will improve your ability to
assert yourself.

✔ Be assertive in your body language. Stand (or sit) tall,
taking up plenty of space. Breathe deeply and easily,
making eye contact with an open expression. Don't
fiddle with your hands or cross your arms or legs.
Clasp your hands lightly, relaxing your shoulders.

✔ Practise projecting your voice strongly. Start by exhaling
all the air in your lungs, which will trigger your body
to take a deep breath before you talk. Enunciate
consonants clearly, keep your voice soft but turn up the
volume. Drop the pitch of your voice (without dropping
the volume) at the end of the phrase to convey your
conviction in your own words.

✔ Until you get used to communicating assertively, you
may want to give yourself time to consider your response

with useful phrases like 'Possibly, I'll get back to you on that', or 'I need to think about that, I'll let you know'.

✔ If people interrupt you while you're talking, raise a hand to signal 'stop', increase the volume slightly and finish your sentence with conviction. If this continues to happen, you can say 'please let me finish' as you put up your hand, to draw the person's attention to what they're doing. Keep your cool and continue your point, 'I was saying that . . .'.

✔ Recognise the other's point of view whilst saying what you think. It's important to express yourself honestly but constructively. A useful phrase could be: 'I realise that you . . . but I feel that . . .'.

✔ When asked to do something, state clearly what your answer is, what you're prepared to do and what you are not. Don't feel that you have to justify yourself; it's the request that you're turning down, not the person. Repeat the message until the other person accepts it and don't be brow beaten.

TOP TIP
Believe in the value of your perspective and opinions: they are valuable. Remind yourself: 'there are many perspectives on any situation and my point of view is worth hearing; people may need my perspective too'.

Step four: Develop stress-busting habits

Biochemicals are released in response to stress to prepare your body for action. If 'fight' or 'flight' aren't required to deal with the situation they may continue to affect the whole body even after the stress has gone. Taking exercise as part of the working day is the single most effective stress reliever. Regular exercise boosts your energy and gives you increased stamina. It removes the effects of the biochemicals adrenaline and cortisol. Exercise will relieve stress: following a stressful meeting, take a brisk walk to burn them off before resuming your day.

A routine that includes aerobic, anaerobic, and stretching exercises is ideal but the best exercise of all is the kind that fits in with your lifestyle. A walk to work, a policy of using the stairs rather than the lift, and a lunchtime stroll are ways to fit exercise into the working day. A Saturday cycle ride and a couple of visits to the gym or exercise class during the week are all it takes to release the noradrenaline and endorphins which relieve the tension caused by a frenetic daily routine. You'll improve your circulation and digestion at the same time, making a good night's sleep more likely.

TOP TIP
Agree with your partner or friends when you want to spend time together and then block it out in the diary. An exercise class is a good

idea since it occurs at a set time and it's a
good social activity if you enjoy time with
others. Even if you spend a relaxing hour in
the bath with some candles and a book,
you'll feel more ready to handle the demands
of others. Say goodbye to 'false friends'.
Cigarettes, coffee, alcohol, and chocolate
are all likely to add to the negative
effects of stress over time. Give them
up and get some help if you need it.

Common mistakes

✗ **You're available 24/7**
Deal with phones and e-mails during set periods of the
day only. Turn off the 'message alert' message on your
computer and turn off your mobile or BlackBerry®
in-between times so that you can concentrate on other
things. This still means that you're giving people a
reasonable response time but in managed chunks of
time that will keep you sane.

✗ **You don't prioritise your e-mails**
With e-mails, a full inbox can be overwhelming, so
start with a trawl through to delete spam and other
unimportant 'noise' from your mail. Then 'classify' the
e-mails that remain: some require an instant response
and some require only a couple of lines and can be
dispatched straight away. File longer e-mails that require
your considered response or ones with reading matter

attached, so that you can give them appropriate attention; make a quick note in your 'To Do' list to remind you. Prioritise the mails that are left and deal with them as effectively as you can.

STEPS TO SUCCESS

✓ Recognise stressful situations and try to plan ahead for them. Identify what you can do to help yourself.

✓ Major life events can knock you for six, especially where several occur in the same two years. Don't isolate yourself—contact with others will help you get back on your feet.

✓ When dealing with difficult behaviour, keep a positive outlook; getting down or angry will not help the situation.

✓ Confront people who are consistently difficult and try to get the relationship on a healthier footing. Describe what the problem is, describe how it affects you and others, describe what you would like to see, and ask what the barriers are.

✓ Know what you want and communicate it assertively. Expect a positive reaction and you'll very often get one if what you're asking for is fair.

✓ Develop healthy habits of exercise and eating. Being in shape will allow you to live life to your full potential.

Useful links

Learn Direct:

www.learndirect.co.uk

Mindtools.com (stress management tab):

www.mindtools.com/smpage.html

Where to find more help

**Downshifting: How to Work Less and Enjoy
It More**
John D. Drake
San Franciso: Berrett-Koehler, 2001
136pp ISBN: 1576751163
This is a thought-provoking book aimed at anyone unhappy with
their current work–life balance. It offers advice to those thinking
of changing their life to a less work-centred one but also gives
time-management help to readers coping with long working
days.

**Find the Balance: Essential Steps to Fulfillment
in Your Work and Life**
Deborah Tom
London: BBC Books, 2004
192pp ISBN 0563521384
It was once thought that a successful career was the key to
achieving happiness, but recent studies have shown that many
people suffer negatively when trying to balance their work and
social life. Through a number of case studies, *Find the Balance*
offers simple solutions to help readers achieve well-being and
fulfillment in all areas of their lives.

Get Everything Done and Still Have Time to Play
Mark Forster
London: Help Yourself Books, 2000
208pp ISBN 0340746203
Based on the author's view that time can't be managed, but that
you can change the way you focus on tasks so that you make the
best use of time available, this book offers advice on how to
prioritise, plan, allocate time-slots to different activities, and
overcome your resistance to some of the demands on your day-to-
day life.

The Joy of Laziness: How to Slow Down and Live Longer

Peter Axt and Michaela Axt-Gadermann
London: Bloomsbury, 2005
160pp ISBN: 0747576769

If you're trying to combat all the many demands on your energy, it may be time to try a different approach: laziness! Based on scientific research, this book explains how much we benefit from taking things easier and how doing 'nothing' actually does a great deal of good. The authors are both former (and reformed) champion athletes and they have written an accessible book aimed at anyone who wants to look and feel healthy, be happy, and live longer.

anger, coping with 77–9
answer phones 72
assertiveness 80–1

benefits, and flexible working 27, 29, 36
breaks, rest 70

career breaks 29, 51–63
    advantages of 47–8
    asking your employer 54–6
    changing your employer 58–9
    financial implications 48, 53–4, 62
    keeping in touch 60, 61–2
    motives for 52–4
    other ways of achieving goals 57–8
    refusal 56–7
    taking the plunge 59–61
    tying up loose ends 61
childcare 47, 48
children, family demands 43–6
communication, assertiveness 80–1
computers 28, 67
control:
    'being in the zone' 6
    in-balance state 5–6, 7
    learning to prioritise 64–73
    locus of 7–9
    out-of-balance state 3–4, 7
    criticism, coping with 76–7

'dead batteries' 79–80
deadlines 66
diaries 8, 12, 21, 66–7, 69, 70
dismissal, unfair 53

e-mails 71, 83–4
exercise 82–3

family demands 40–50
    advantages of not working 47–8

compatibility with work role 46–7
    identifying 43–6
finances:
    career breaks 48, 53–4, 62
    flexible working 36
    working abroad 58
flexi-time working 26
flexible working 25–39
    applying for 29–33, 35–6, 48
    financial implications 36
    options 26–9
    setting up systems 33–5

goals see objectives

home working 28, 37–8, 57
housework 43–6, 47

in-balance state 5–6, 7
inputs, managing 69–72
Internet, home working 28
isolation 37–8, 57

job sharing 27

life events, stress 75–6, 84
locus of control 7–9

maternity leave 26, 59
milestones 67, 68
motivation 21–2, 23

needs, other people's 23
negotiations:
    career breaks 54–6
    flexible working 29–33, 35–6, 48

objectives 19–22
    career breaks 52
    learning to prioritise 65–6
    managing inputs and outputs 69–70
out-of-balance state 3–4, 7

outputs, managing 69–70
overseas work 58

parental leave 26, 58–9
part-time working 27, 57
partners, family demands 40–1, 43–6
phone calls 71–2, 83
planning:
    diaries 66–7, 69, 70
    3–1–6–1 plans 19–21
    To Do lists 67–8, 69, 70
post, dealing with 70–1
pregnancy 26, 58–9
priorities:
    and career breaks 52–3
    and values 12–24
prioritisation 64–73
    objectives 65–6
    tools 66–9
productivity 2, 32
project planners 68

redundancy 53–4
relationships, stress 76–80
relaxation 46, 75–6
role confusion 69

sabbaticals see career breaks
sick leave 2, 32
skills, career breaks and 60, 61–2
software, time management 67

stress 2, 74–85
    assertive communication 80–1
    relationships 76–80
    sources of 74–6
    stress-busting habits 82–3

telephones 71–2, 83
teleworking 28, 57
term-time working 28
time audits 68
time management, diaries 66–7, 69, 70
time out 46
To Do lists 67–8, 69, 70
training, after career breaks 60
trapped, feeling 10
travel 58

unfair dismissal 53

values 12–24
    and goals 19–22
    hierarchy of 16–18
    other people's 22
visas, working abroad 58

work permits, working abroad 58
work role:
    advantages and demands of 41–2
    advantages of not working 47–8
    compatibility with family demands 46–7